Phil Moser can be summed up in two words: biblical and practical. He is a master at applying the Scriptures to everyday issues in such a way that people walk away with lives changed.

KEVIN O'BRIEN
Pastor, Ocean City Baptist Church

Phil Moser has done an admirable job of identifying spiritual principles and then applying them to daily life. I commend this work both to those struggling with their daily walk, and to those counselors who are seeking additional tools.

DR. JOHN MACARTHUR
Pastor-Teacher, Grace Community Church
President, The Master's Seminary

Hats off to Phil Moser for helping us navigate through life's most challenging issues in a clearly biblical way. The thing I like about these booklets is that they are forged by a pastor who has successfully wrestled through these issues with his flock, and thankfully he now shares them with the church at large.

DR. JOE STOWELL
President, Cornerstone University

It has been a high privilege to know Phil Moser for more than 20 years. He is one of today's most gifted communicators; possessing an unusual ability to deliver biblical truth in an intensely personal and practical way. Our guests and students rate him a perennial favorite. I can give no higher recommendation for your next conference or speaking opportunity.

DON LOUGH
Executive Director, Word of Life Fellowship

Pastor Phil's writing reflects a deep commitment to helping individuals both understand and obey God's Word in their daily life. As an experienced counselor he realizes that just teaching the truth is not enough; people need help on the practical steps of disciplining themselves for the purpose of godliness. I commend this combination of exposition, call to obedience and "how-to."

RANDY PATTEN
Director of Training and Advancement
Association of Certified Biblical Counselors

As an educator, Phil Moser is distinctively gifted. His pedagogical skill enables him to clearly explain very difficult concepts in understandable language that all learners can grasp. Audiences would greatly benefit by his teaching.

CAROL A. SHARP, PH.D.
Served as Dean of the College of Education 2002-2012
Rowan University, Glassboro, New Jersey

I have been greatly encouraged by Phil's teaching. When I listen to him, I always walk away with more. More knowledge, more insight, more understanding, more hope. He's my go-to-guy when I have questions about the Bible or Christian living.

MICHAEL BOGGS
Singer-Songwriter
Winner of Multiple Dove Awards

The Biblical Strategies materials have been a big plus for our adult classes. With the inclusion of the memory verse packs and accountability study guides, the materials lend themselves readily to the discipleship process.

STEVE WILLOUGHBY
Pastor, First Baptist Church of Patchogue, New York

Strength for the Struggle

biblical strategies
for standing against
sexual temptation

Phil Moser

Strength for the Struggle: biblical strategies for standing against sexual temptation

Published by Biblical Strategies.
Distributed by Send the Light.

Visit our Web site: www.biblicalstrategies.com.

© 2015 Phil Moser
International Standard Book Number: 978-0-9905666-6-3

Credits:
Cover Art: Gary Lizzi
Cover Photograph: Julie Moore
Copy Editor: Justin Carlton

Contributions:
A special thanks to Kevin Bult for his testimony of accountability.

Note: You may download a free accountability plan/study guide for *Strength for the Struggle* by visiting biblicalstrategies.com. Choose the resource tab to print the guide and other tools.

CONTENTS

THE TALE OF TWO GIANTS

Circa 1040 BC

THE BELLOWING of the giant echoed across the valley floor. The boy-king looked down into the Brook of Elah. Shimmering waters rolled over the small stones at the waters' edge. Undeterred by the giant's size, strength, or reputation, the boy-king picked up five small stones and slipped them into his shepherd's bag. These were not your typical rocks for child's play. They were barium sulphate—twice the density of normal stones. When launched from his sling at 100 m.p.h. they would have the stopping power of a .45 caliber handgun.[1] At nearly ten feet tall, the giant appeared invincible, but appearances can be deceiving. The boy-king had five stones and the skill of a sniper. He raised his voice in answer to the giant's intimidation:

> *This day the Lord will deliver you into my hand, and I will strike you down! That all this assembly may know that the Lord saves not with sword and spear. For the battle is the Lord's and he will give you into our hands!* [2]

Goliath was out of his league. And on that spring day, while thousands looked on, the giant fell to the little-boy-king named David.

Circa 1015 BC

Twenty-five years have passed. The boy-king has become a man. He's looking down again, but it's not for five small stones to slay a giant. David is on the roof of his palace, and his eyes scan the rooftops below. He knows what he's looking for, though he's acting like he doesn't. He's seen her bathing once before; the image keeps returning to his mind—beckoning him to forbidden pleasures. *It's only a glance*, he reasons. *If she appears, I'll look away.* Suddenly she's there, on her rooftop—just as if his memory had called the image to life. His pulse quickens. His breathing comes quick and shallow. He knows what's next—the memory of those past images awakening his desire. He turns his head away, but his eyes reach back toward the woman bathing. A battle ensues.

Look away. She's not your wife.

It's just a glance. No one will see you.

This is wrong. You're a married man.

You're free tonight. Is she?

Transfixed—his body's stillness does not reveal his mind's struggle. The internal battle is fast and furious; his will weakening under the onslaught. What had started as curiosity is now the full grown desire for pleasure. His imagination is racing ahead with the images he has captured. Entitlement is not far behind: *You're the king! What's wrong with looking...since you're the king and she's your subject? Find out her name and invite her to the castle.*

There once was a boy-king who, with five small stones and a sling, watched a giant fall and gave God the glory. But when he became a man, he chose to stand unarmed on the top of his palace, locked in a life-and-death struggle with the giant of sexual desire. This time, the giant didn't bellow intimidating curses across the valley floor. It whispered promises of unrealized pleasure—of being desired and desiring in return. And on that spring day, the giant won the battle, defeating the king who had pursued his own pleasure, and at great cost to the kingdom.[3]

THINK LIKE GOD THINKS
Five Small Stones

K ING DAVID was a man after God's own heart, yet his temptation with Bathsheba revealed a lack of the kind of character he exhibited when he was younger. God had chosen him as king (instead of one of his older brothers) for his purity of heart.[4] However, as his story unfolded, those key inner qualities that he once possessed began to fade. While the compromises may have seemed small at first, they left him vulnerable in his battle with sexual temptation.

After 25 years of listening, learning, and guiding people through the regret and devastation of sexual failures, I've discovered that their stories have common touch points. Like David, the individuals I encounter also lack an internal fortitude to strengthen their will when temptation beckons with sexual desires. I'd like for you to imagine those inner qualities as "five small stones." Just as David reached into the brook and gathered five stones to slay Goliath, these inner qualities are powerful weapons to be utilized in our battle for sexual purity. As a young man, David practiced them with proficiency. He was as internally accurate as he was externally—he could hit the target of temptation, just as he struck Goliath. But if you could do a postmortem on David's adulterous relationship with Bathsheba, you would see that, later in life, his spiritual sling lacked projectiles. Those five key qualities—so essential to his battle with sexual temptation—had fallen into disuse. In that moment, David was an unarmed warrior. For each of us, these stones are just as valuable when we battle sexual temptation. With them, we can stand against desire. Without them, just like David, we'll fall.

Humility

To walk in humility is to recognize that you cannot win the battle with sexual temptation in your own strength.

Integrity

To practice integrity is to make a commitment to transparency during temptation, and to confession after sin.

Loyalty

To desire loyalty is to love God by using your body for his glory, not your temporary pleasure.

Responsibility

To exercise responsibility limits your opportunity for temptation because you are preoccupied fulfilling your commitments.

Accountability

To live with accountability is to guard your vulnerabilities through the Word and fellow believers.

Stone #1: Humility

> To walk in humility is to recognize that you cannot win the battle with sexual temptation in your own strength.

If I could choose only one internal quality to help men and women stand against sexual temptation, it would be humility. Humble people lack the sense of entitlement that makes them vulnerable to temptation. They do not presume upon their own spiritual strength. They deny themselves the credit for past successes. But, most importantly, they do not believe they have the wherewithal to stand against sexual temptation on their own. When tempted, they prefer Joseph's burst of speed to loitering in sin's vicinity:

> She [Potiphar's wife] kept putting pressure on Joseph day after day, but he refused to sleep with her, and he kept out of her way as much as possible. One day, however, no one else was around when he went in to do his work. She came and grabbed him by his cloak, demanding, "Come on, sleep with me!" Joseph tore himself away, but he left his cloak in her hand *as he ran from the house* [emphasis added].[5]

In the early stages of David's life, he demonstrated a Joseph-like humility. He certainly had reasons to succumb to pride. He was skilled in music and speech, he was a courageous warrior and an anointed king, and he was good looking too![6] His victory over Goliath made him the subject of the Jewish songwriters and dancers.[7] But great accomplishments themselves do not make one prideful; they only reveal whether humility or pride resides within. In those early years, David was quick to declare that his strength was in the Lord, not in his ability. His humility is revealed in his in verbal sparring with the giant Goliath:

> This day the Lord will deliver you into my hand, and
> I will strike you down [...] that all this assembly may
> know that the Lord saves not with sword and spear.
> For the battle is the Lord's, and he will give you into
> our hand.[8]

Earlier, David had been in a skirmish with a lion and a bear, and he knew that the Lord had delivered him.[9] He was confident that this battle would have the same outcome. A warrior in God's hand was an instrument, he reasoned, not unlike the sling in his own.

Walking in humility and being humiliated are two very different things. Walking in humility is proactive while being humiliated is a reaction to feeling shame. Because both help us see sin for what it is, they are sometimes mistaken for one another. Both the unfaithful spouse and the teenager struggling with pornography are equally humiliated when they are found out. In the moment of their embarrassment, they see it for what it is: a costly, stupid choice.[10] Being humbled in the moment, however, is no assurance that you will walk in humility once the shame fades. It may serve as a short-term protection, but learning to walk in humility is the secret to being victorious beyond that moment. Like David, walking in humility is the moment-by-moment effort to remember your weakness and reflect on God's strength.

Living in light of your weakness

To walk in humility means that you won't presume upon your own spiritual strength. Notice the warnings of Scripture regarding sexual temptation:

- Run from sexual sin! No other sin so clearly affects the body as this one does.[11]

- But you, Timothy, are a man of God; so run from

all these evil things. Pursue righteousness and a godly life.[12]

- Run from anything that stimulates youthful lusts. Instead, pursue righteous living, faithfulness, love, and peace.[13]

The New Testament commands echo the Old Testament actions of Joseph. Both reveal an understanding of personal weakness. When it comes to sexual desires, only a fool would think he possesses the will-power to overcome temptation.

During my high school years, I opened the newspaper one morning to read of a nationally recognized religious leader whose adulterous relationship had been exposed. I was incredulous. I had read the man's books and learned from them. I shook my head in disbelief—*how could that happen to him?* Years later in graduate school, I heard the rest of the story. Whenever this man would speak away from his home, he would often receive a knock on his hotel door. Upon answering, he would find a woman requesting counsel in light of his ministry earlier that evening. For years, this man had maintained a pattern of never releasing the three-inch security chain on his hotel door. Whatever brief counsel he would give would always be through that three-inch opening. Then one day he broke that pattern. There was nothing inherently sinful in the counsel that was given that night, but the emotional relationship that ensued would later lead to adultery. The image of that three-inch chain has remained with me through the years. There is both physical and emotional distance maintained through that opening. To release it is to lack humility. It is an act of spiritual arrogance. It says, "This may be a dangerous situation for others, but it is not for me." And if, as in this Christian leader's case, you do not fall the first time you cross the line of your personal limits, the moment has served to further embolden the prideful notion that you won't fall the next time.[14] This is why the Bible warns us to flee sexual temptation. To run from temptation is to walk in humility.

Seeking the wisdom of God

Prayer is man's vocalization of spiritual weakness. By it, we acknowledge that we are in need of God's help. This is our first stop in the quest for humility. Catherine Marshall wrote,

> Admittance to the school of prayer is by an entrance test with only two questions. The first one is: Are you in real need? The second is: Do you admit that you are helpless to handle that need? Why would God insist upon helplessness as a prerequisite to answered prayer? One obvious reason is because our human helplessness is a bed-rock fact. God is a realist and insists that we be realists too. So long as we are deluding ourselves that human resources can supply our heart's desires, we are believing a lie.[15]

In David's early life, when facing a significant decision, we read that he "inquired of the Lord."[16] While he doesn't lack confidence in his decisions, he is intentional about knowing what God wants prior to taking steps forward. His "inquiry" reveals a dependence on the Lord for wisdom. His regular dependence on God's wisdom testifies to his humility. Sadly, the phrase "inquired of the Lord" disappears from David's story six chapters before his moral failure with Bathsheba. Coincidence? I doubt it. David had stopped seeking the wisdom of the Lord in humble dependence for some time prior to his adultery. Prayer as a first response to challenges reveals a humble heart. It is our testimony to an all-powerful God that we recognize our personal strength is not enough.

David's outward pattern of prayer revealed an inner posture of dependence. The humble-hearted person seeks God's wisdom because he believes he lacks it. On the contrary, the prideful-hearted is confident he knows more than he really does. Hence, he misses warnings from the Word and caution from others. If you're struggling with sexual sin, seek God's wisdom in prayer (page 60).

Living by the strength of God

When we call out to the Lord in prayer, we are acknowledging that his strength is superior to our own. But how are we to attain that strength? One of the ways we live in light of God's strength is to familiarize ourselves with the character of God. David did this throughout the Psalms. Notice the words that communicate who God is to him:

> I love you, O Lord, my *strength*. The Lord is my *rock* and my *fortress* and my *deliverer*, my God, my *rock*, in whom I take *refuge*, my *shield*, and the horn of my s*alvation*, my *stronghold* [emphasis added].[17]

While the humble person acknowledges his own moral weakness, he also finds courage in rehearsing God's moral strength. The one walking in humility thinks this way: *If I attempted this in my own strength, I would fail. But when I remember that God is my deliverer, shield, and strength, I believe that I can overcome this sin.*

In our struggle with sin, we must remember that we cannot live by the strength of God if we are not rehearsing the attributes of God. If you're going to reach for the strength of God when you're tempted, you'll need to acquire your knowledge of him beforehand.

A good friend of mine served in the Marines. During training, he had to take a apart his weapon, clean it, and put it back together again. That doesn't sound so difficult, does it? But there was a catch. There were 15 steps in the process, and he had less than 30 seconds to complete the exercise in the dark. A marine's success in battle was directly linked to his preparation prior to the battle. The same is true in the spiritual realm. To walk in humility, you can't simply rely on your own strength: you must know intimately the strength of God. You develop that knowledge by rehearsing the character of God during times of peace, not during the heat of battle. Daily meditating upon an attribute or quality of God is a great way to do pre-battle training. You will find a 30-day listing of God's attributes at biblicalstrategies.com under the resource tab.

Acknowledgement of personal weakness should cause us to reach for a source of strength outside of ourselves. The Christian finds that source of strength in the character of God. Rehearsing the ways that God is strong—when we are not—and making decisions in light of those truths when we're tempted is another step in our walk of humility.

Stone # 2: Integrity

To practice integrity is to make a commitment to transparency during temptation, and to confession after sin.

Learning to lie is an essential part of remaining trapped in sexual sin. Unfortunately, we become fairly adept at lying long before we struggle with sexual temptation. Even in our toddler years, when we crossed over lines our parents drew, we looked for ways to cover it up. During our teenage years, we become even more proficient at hiding things we knew were wrong. It didn't take the internet search engines long to discover that what their clientele wanted was "private browsing" or ways to go "incognito." This was the allure behind the Ashley Madison website, which promised its patrons it would keep their desire for an illicit affair private—until hackers broke through and revealed their clients to the entire world.[18] But having your dirty laundry aired publicly is not the only downside to your dishonesty. David labored hard to cover his adulterous relationship with Bathsheba; once it became public, however, his confession revealed that there had been another price to pay:

> Blessed is the man against whom the Lord counts no iniquity, and in whose spirit there is no deceit. *For when I kept silent, my bones wasted away through my groaning all day long. For day and night your hand was heavy upon me; my strength was dried up as by the heat of summer* [emphasis added].[19]

David acknowledged that the effort it took to keep sin hidden nearly undid him. When a friend of our family became aware of her spouse's sexual sin, she said "the truth didn't kill me, but the lies nearly did." While dishonesty has a devastating effect on the victim, it has a similar effect on the perpetrator. They carry the secret alone, and the guilt can be unbearable.

During my years as a pastor, I have seen this effect on those I counsel. Dealing with the guilt has often led them to a host of temporary remedies. Whether they abuse alcohol or prescription meds, they experience the harsh reality: when the high wears off, the guilt remains. They carry the secret day and night.

In the same Psalm, David reveals that, once a sin has been committed, the person of integrity should know that confession is his best option going forward:

> Blessed is the one whose transgression is forgiven, whose sin is covered [...] I acknowledged my sin to you, and I did not cover my iniquity; I said, "I will confess my transgressions to the Lord," and you forgave the iniquity of my sin.[20]

One of the strongest deterrents against sexual sin is integrity—both transparency during temptation, and confession after the sin.

There is another danger to deceit. Because lying is a means of avoiding the immediate consequences of your actions, it develops quickly into a habit and becomes your first response to conflict. While David's heart was pure as a young man, his dishonest ways began long before he discovered Bathsheba was pregnant with his child.

We lie when we fear the consequences of truth-telling

David's first recorded lie took place years earlier when he feared for his life. The reigning king, Saul, was jealous of young David's popularity. Saul had, on more than one occasion, attempted to take David's life,[21] fearing his young protégé's popularity.[22] Jonathan (Saul's son) and David developed a scheme to determine the seriousness of the present danger. The scheme didn't depend upon deceit, but included it. In his fear, David felt that additional detail—while untrue—would keep him safe as he hid in a nearby field. David had Jonathan tell Saul that he had returned home to Bethlehem.[23] It seems like a minor detail, but this is the first of three lies that David tells in rapid fashion—a poignant reminder to how quickly lying becomes a habit. As opposed to trusting God and telling the truth, David feared the consequences that would come if his location were discovered. He chose lying as his means of protection.

We lie when we fear our secret may be exposed

Because the threat of Saul's assault was real, David fled. At his first stop, the city of Nob, he lied again—this time to the priest of the city, Ahimelech. On this occasion, David fears exposure of his secret. Ahimelech asks: "Why are you alone, and no one is with you?"[24] David responds with a tale about Saul sending him on a secret mission, insisting he tell no one. None of this is true, of course, but it temporarily keeps the truth—that Saul is out to kill him—a secret. This is a lie with tremendous consequence for others: it will later result in the death of 85 priests and an entire city—a city unaware that they were housing a fugitive.[25] The lie David told to guard against the exposure of his secret works for him but is costly for others. Rarely does a secret remain a secret—especially when sin is involved.

We lie with our actions, not only our words

David's third lie follows on the heels of his first two. In his fear of Saul, he runs to a Philistine city. But soon, those in that city recognize him as the one who killed the Philistine warrior, Goliath. Fearing for his future, David feigns that he has gone mad. Lying can be both verbal and nonverbal. When it comes to hiding sexual sin, it is often the latter. We go about acting like everything is fine, when it is not.

Lying, like gambling, has two dangers. The first is that it will cost us. But the second, and greater danger is that we'll be successful at it. Success breeds the confidence that we should try it again.

Stone #3: Loyalty

> To desire loyalty is to love God by using your
> body for his glory, not your temporary pleasure.

On the cover of this book, you'll see a sling with five stones. At first glance, it is often mistaken for four. The darker colored one is uniquely positioned, behind the others. The cover serves as a visual reminder that one stone—the stone of loyalty—is set apart from the others. Loyalty is the quality that is working in the background; the one quality that supports all the others. Loyalty is the word that best communicates your ongoing relationship with God. This relationship is foundational to being able to successfully practice humility, integrity, responsibility, and accountability. Following David's admission of his adultery with Bathsheba and his murder of her husband, he pens two Psalms of confession.[26] In one of them he writes,

> Create in me a clean heart, O God. Renew a *loyal*
> spirit within me[...] Restore to me the joy of your
> salvation, and make me willing to obey you
> [emphasis added].[27]

The word *loyal* means "steadfast, established or enduring."[28] Perhaps you have a friend or family member whose name comes to mind when you hear the word loyal. Here, David is acknowledging that his loyalty to God is need of renewal. One writer has said of David's confession,

> David wasn't content just to mutter a quick 'forgive
> me for all my sins.' His repentance was thorough and
> earnest. ... He sees his sins depriving him of his stead-
> fastness in the Lord's ways, and longs to have that
> changed.[29]

When a soldier goes off to war, his action is perceived as an expression of loyalty to his country. Perhaps he is motivated to protect his family or community; nonetheless, loyalty for the soldier might mean he will pay the ultimate price. Indeed, to jump sides in the heat of battle (in order to save his own life) would be an act of disloyalty. Such an action would earn that man labels of coward, traitor, defector, or deserter. In war time, loyalty, taken to its ultimate conclusion, means willingness to sacrifice your body on behalf of the cause.

In the early stages of David's military career, he had such loyalty. He exhibited a willingness to place himself in harm's way for the highest cause of all: the glory of God. On the battle field with Goliath he declared:

> The Lord who delivered me from the paw of the lion and from the paw of the bear will deliver me from the hand of this Philistine. [...] This day the Lord will deliver you into my hand, [...] that all the earth may know that there is a God in Israel.[30]

Whenever God's glory was at stake, David jumped in with a willingness to die if necessary. Whether the antagonist was a lion, a bear or a giant, he was wholly dependent on God for deliverance.

In his post-adultery confession, David longed for the *loyal spirit* he once had. Somewhere, in some way, he'd lost the thing he'd once possessed. His consuming desire to glorify God, his willingness to sacrifice his very life for the cause, was gone. In its place was the consuming desire to please self. Sexual sin is a cruel taskmaster. It promises *once is enough*, but never keeps that promise. The pages of Scripture reference David's multiple wives,[31] but three receive his special attention: Abigail, Michael, and Bathsheba. Sadly, each of these women were married to another man when David desired them.[32]

Let that thought settle in. In the early stages of his life, David would have sacrificed his very life for God's glory.

But his repeated surrender to sexual temptation had weakened his resolve. In that void, he would actually justify the taking of another's life so that he could have what he desired and not suffer any consequences for it.[33] When it came to Goliath, he fought valiantly, but when it came to sexual desire, he succumbed readily. David's failure teaches us a vital lesson. The battle he lost with his sexual desires was not the result of too much testosterone. It was the product of shifting loyalties. A heart that had once fully desired God now sought other pleasures. The proverbs warn us of this danger: *Guard your heart above all else, for it determines the course of your life.*[34] With his heart destabilized, David's desires determined his choices instead of his loyalty. He did things he would have never done before.

Furthermore, his choices with Bathsheba revealed another change: whom he would choose to serve with his body. He chose his personal pleasure over God's glory. The New Testament further reminds us that our body is best used for God's glory rather than our personal pleasure. In one of the most definitive passages in the Bible on sexual temptation we read the following:

> Flee from sexual immorality. Every other sin a person commits is outside the body, but *the sexually immoral person sins against his own body*. Or do you not know that your body is a temple of the Holy Spirit within you, whom you have from God? *You are not your own, for you were bought with a price. So glorify God in your body* [emphasis added].[35]

In order to battle sexual temptation effectively, we must answer the question: *whom will I glorify with my body?* David's choices reveal a failure to answer that question properly. He assumed his body was for his personal use. Where he had previously used his body for the glory of God, he now became a defector, siding instead with his personal pleasure.[36] He joined up with the side that defended his fleshly desires rather than sacrificed them. From the Bible's perspective, the most important axiom in your battle with sexual temptation—and often the most forgotten—is this:

Until your desire for the glory of God surpasses your desire for sexual gratification you will be unable to stand against sexual temptation.

Read that statement again, slowly. Real strength in the struggle with sexual temptation is drawn from an intense loyalty to God and his glory. David, with his shifting loyalties, had forgotten that truth. Previously, he had trumpeted the glory of God in nearly 80 Psalms bearing his name, but all that was forgotten in the quagmire of desire.

The Scriptures describe the believer's body as a *temple*.[37] Like a temple, your body was intended to function as a vessel for giving God glory. In pursuing his glory, you will find a richer motivation; one that dwarfs the giant of your sexual desires. It's hard to pursue God's glory and forbidden pleasures at the same time.

The Bitterroot Valley in Montana is home to five mountain ranges. Because the valley is so vast, you have uninterrupted vision in any direction. The beauty of each sunrise is reflected by that entire range of mountains. In a recent visit there, as I watched the sunrise color those mountains, my imagination was captured by the glory of God. Neither words nor pictures can describe what I saw—the beauty of those mountains is something to be experienced. Seeing God's creation like that made it easy to worship him. As I attempted to grasp the enormity of that country, I *felt* small. Gandalf the Grey's words to the three-

and-a-half-foot tall Bilbo Baggins captures this idea:

> You don't really suppose, do you, that all your adventures and escapes were managed by mere luck, just for your sole benefit? You are a very fine person, Mr. Baggins, and I am very fond of you; *but you are only quite a little fellow in a wide world after all!* "Thank goodness!" said Bilbo laughing [emphasis added].[38]

Bilbo breathes a sigh of relief when he realizes the world does not revolve around him. Likewise, we are relieved when we realize that the entire world is not about us! Consistently reflecting on the glory of God brings that perspective. The gravitas of God's glory shrinks you and me—and our desires—down to size. In the shadow of his glory, my sexual desires don't seem like badly behaved giants I can't control. It's just not possible to maintain a sense of entitlement when you're standing in awe of the glory of God.

The Bible further reminds us that our worship of God is uniquely tied to what we do with our bodies. It is this perspective that Paul brings to bear:

> And so, dear brothers and sisters, I plead with you to *give your bodies to God because of all he has done for you.* Let them be a living and holy sacrifice—the kind he will find acceptable. This is truly the way to worship him. Don't copy the behavior and customs of this world, but let God transform you into a new person by changing the way you think. Then you will learn to know God's will for you, which is good and pleasing and perfect [emphasis added].[39]

This is the truth David forgot: *until your desire for the glory of God surpasses your desire for sexual gratification you will be unable to stand against sexual temptation.* As we meditate on the glory of God, our focus is drawn to him. His glory becomes the divine protection in our battle with sexual sin.

Stone #4: Responsibility

> To exercise responsibility limits your opportunity
> for temptation because you are preoccupied
> fulfilling your commitments.

The chapter in the Bible that details David's sexual sin
with Bathsheba begins with a vital piece of information:

> In the spring of the year, *when kings normally go out to*
> *war*, David sent Joab and the Israelite army to fight...
> However, David stayed behind in Jerusalem. *Late one*
> *afternoon, after his midday rest*, David got out of bed and
> was walking on the roof of the palace [emphasis
> added].[40]

At a time when David should have been protecting his
country from those who would do it harm, he sent someone
else to do the job. Furthermore, while the Israeli army was
posting a watch, alert to enemy movement, David was just
waking up from an afternoon nap. The significance of these
phrases cannot be overemphasized. David is not engaged in
the areas for which he is responsible. This wasn't a one-
time dereliction of duty: it had become a pattern in David's
life that made him vulnerable to sexual temptation.

A number of years ago, I read of a survey where men
had been asked what day of the week they most often engaged in viewing pornography and fulfilled those desires
through self-gratification. The vast majority referenced
Friday and Saturday night. While sexual temptation does-
n't single out any particular day, it does seem to be
uniquely tied to one's work week. The acceleration of sexual desires is tied to your thought life, so when your
thoughts are actively engaged in other responsibilities
throughout the week, you are less prone for your mind to
wander into forbidden terrain.[41]

When my older children became young adults, I routinely warned them: *your free time is enemy territory.*[42]

We should be more alert when we come off the clock or end our work week. Perhaps during those times we drop our mental guard, or maybe our sense of entitlement to relaxation is elevated after a long day/week. Whatever the case, when David had taken time off from his routine responsibilities, he was primed to be tempted when he spied Bathsheba bathing.

Young adults are uniquely susceptible to this dangerous reality. From them, I've often heard comments like, "I didn't have anything else to do" or "I was bored" offered as reasons for succumbing to sexual temptation. We can learn a lesson from David here: *responsibility limits opportunity for temptation as you are preoccupied fulfilling your commitments.*

For a straightforward reminder of our responsibilities, the Christian can turn to the New Testament epistles. These brief letters offer a unique combination of theology and practical living. In particular, the epistle to the Colossians offers *responsibility* reminders in three areas: family, work and ministry. It has been my experience as a pastor that when people fail to give effort in these areas, they often open the door wider to sexual temptation.

1. Family Responsibilities

> Wives, submit to your husbands, as is fitting in the Lord. Husbands, love your wives, and do not be harsh with them. Children, obey your parents in everything, for this pleases the Lord. Fathers, do not provoke your children, lest they become discouraged.[43]

Each of us bears certain responsibilities in the home. In this passage, we are charged to exercise mutual love and support in the husband/wife relationship, and care and obedience in the parent/child relationship. Whether we work or go to school, we can come home at the end of the day thinking we've fulfilled our responsibilities. It is our home after all. I know that at the end of my workday, it's easy to believe it's all about me. My time. My comfort. My peace and quiet. And my remote control. How quickly I forget that my responsibilities as a husband and a father don't diminish when I walk in the back door. They intensify. Subtly, my heart diverts my focus away from my family responsibilities toward the rest and relaxation I think I deserve. David's failure should serve as a powerful reminder: *when he was not fulfilling his responsibilities he was prone to sexual temptation.*

2. Work Responsibilities

> Bondservants, obey in everything those who are your earthly masters, not by way of eye-service, as people-pleasers, but with sincerity of heart, fearing the Lord. Whatever you do, work heartily, as for the Lord and not for men, knowing that from the Lord you will receive the inheritance as your reward. You are serving the Lord Christ [...] Masters, treat your bondservants justly and fairly, knowing that you also have a Master in heaven.[44]

Working hard, even when others aren't watching, is a great trait for any believer to have. But it is especially helpful for the one battling sexual temptation. It reveals that you aren't simply working for your boss's approval, but for God's. Daily practice of that truth serves to protect us from sexual temptation too. Here's why: if your nine-to-five work week is performed under the ever-watchful eye of the Lord, then so is every moment of your weekend. Furthermore, if you have not given your best effort at work and merely acted as though you have—because you believe no one is watching—you are prone to practice the same charade regarding immoral behavior during your free time.

On the positive side, it is deeply fulfilling when your work is well done—even if it isn't recognized this side of heaven. This passage reminds us that, while others may not have noticed your effort here, you can anticipate receiving a reward from the Lord. Think of it this way: *delayed recognition regarding your work performance prepares you to practice delayed gratification regarding your sexual desires.* Delaying in both events—until the God-appointed time—is commended by the Lord.[45]

3. Volunteer/Ministry Responsibilities

Continue steadfastly in prayer, being watchful in it with thanksgiving. At the same time, pray also for us, that God may open to us a door for the word, to declare the mystery of Christ, on account of which I am in prison— that I may make it clear, which is how I ought to speak. Walk in wisdom toward outsiders, making the best use of the time. Let your speech always be gracious, seasoned with salt, so that you may know how you ought to answer each person.[46]

When we are busy living for ourselves, we will not see the opportunities to help others around us. Here, the apostle Paul was requesting prayer for his ministry and encouraging them to participate as well. Volunteering and helping others sounds optional, but when Jesus told the story of the Good Samaritan, he reminded each of us that a hurting brother is a responsibility, not a possibility.[47]

Serving others does more than fill up your time and keep you busy. Like physical labor is good for the body, so serving others is good for the soul. There is a sense of fulfillment and accomplishment when we've helped others well.

Prior to his moral failure, David had grown slack with his responsibilities. We have listed three biblical responsibilities that should help keep you out of trouble, but a more comprehensive approach may be necessary. In the back of this book, you will find a chart with 22 various responsibilities and key Scriptures to study further (page 72). When you fulfill your God-given responsibilities, you are doing more than just staying busy. You will also discover a long-term purpose that surpasses short-term pleasure.

Stone #5: Accountability

> To live with accountability is to guard your vulnerabilities through the Word and your fellow believers.

Accountability is the final stone to help you stand against sexual temptation. The one being held accountable voluntarily surrenders his right to privacy because he understands that not doing so is to court failure. While accountability is a valuable means of protection, it is not intended to stand alone. It is best used in conjunction with the other qualities—humility, integrity, loyalty, and responsibility. Spiritual accountability is provided through two means: the Scriptures and fellow believers.

Accountability through the Scriptures

In the 19th Psalm, David gives six benefits of meditating on the Word of God. Two of those benefits have direct application to accountability:

> The commandment of the Lord is *pure*, enlightening the eyes […] the decrees of the Lord are *true*, and righteous all together […] Moreover, by them your

servant is warned, in keeping them there is great reward. Who can discern his errors? Declare me innocent from hidden faults. Keep back your servant from presumptuous sins; let them not have dominion over me.[48]

Sexual temptation has a fondness for employing deception as its means of attack. The lies come fast and furious. *No one will ever know. It's just one time. It's your body, you can do what you please. You're not hurting anybody else. If two consenting adults love each other, then...*

Because the Word of God is "pure" and "true," it is able to help those struggling with sexual temptation see through that kind of deception prior to falling into sin. In this way, the Scriptures provide a pre-fall means of accountability. Like a good friend by your side, the Word speaks truth to you when you're tempted. It also brings conviction for those who, through repeated failure, have become hardened to their sin. For this reason, the Bible is an excellent—though often overlooked—accountability tool. The writer of Hebrews points this out:

> For the word of God is living and active, sharper than any two-edged sword, piercing to the division of soul and of spirit, of joints and of marrow, and discerning the thoughts and intentions of the heart.[49]

We develop this accountability relationship with the Word when we spend time reading, memorizing, and applying it. Chuck Swindoll says that Scripture memory is the most underused spiritual resource of today's Christian. Don Whitney makes the same case when he writes the following:

> The Word of God is the "sword of the Spirit," but the Holy Spirit cannot give you a weapon you have not stored in the armory of your mind. Imagine yourself

in the midst of a decision and needing guidance, or struggling with a difficult temptation and needing victory. The Holy Spirit rushes to your mental arsenal, flings open the door, but all He finds is a John 3:16, a Genesis 1:1, and a Great Commission. Those are great swords, but they're not made for every battle.[50]

This is why, at the back of every Biblical Strategies booklet, you will find a daily Bible reading schedule, key verses to memorize, and helps for applying the Scriptures to your particular struggle. I encourage you to extend the helpfulness of this book by maintaining those daily practices (for additional help, you can download the accountability plan/ study guide for free under the resources tab at biblical strategies.com). The Word of God is an excellent resource for accountability. But in order for it to accomplish that purpose, you will need to consistently spend time with it.

Strong spiritual relationships with fellow believers will also provide that much needed accountability. Two men in David's life provided that kind of accountability-relationship: Jonathan and Samuel. Sadly, both of these men died early on in David's political career. While David was not responsible for their loss of life, he was responsible for not replacing these relationships with like-minded men.

Accountability requires commitment

There are few relationships in the Bible that compare to the mutual commitment that David and Jonathan had for one another. From the moment of their first meeting we read, "Then Jonathan made a covenant with David, because he loved him as his own soul."[51] Jonathan was willing to place his own life on the line with his angry and mentally unstable father, Saul, in an attempt to protect David's life.[52]

While he would have been heir to the throne, he willingly surrendered that opportunity due to his friendship with David.

Having experienced these types of relationships in my own life, I can attest to their value and closeness. We are humbled by the chance to love someone and know that we are loved by them in return. After Jonathan was killed in battle, David memorializes their friendship in song:

> How the mighty have fallen in the midst of the battle! Jonathan lies slain on your high places. I am distressed for you, my brother Jonathan; very pleasant have you been to me; your love to me was extraordinary, surpassing the love of women.[53]

Accountability that is spiritual in nature

Samuel first met David as a young man, when God had sent the prophet to discover Saul's replacement. While Samuel initially saw the anointing of David as a political appointment, God made it known that he had a far more spiritual reason for the anointing of this young king.[54]

Several years later, when David was in need of physical protection and spiritual direction, he turned to Samuel the prophet for both.[55] Other passages reference the spiritual nature of David's relationship with Samuel and how David depended on Samuel for spiritual direction and counsel. David and Samuel teach us that, to be effective, accountability must be more than just a friend extending comfort in your repeated moral failure.[56] In his book *Finally Free*, biblical counselor Heith Lambert gives seven insights into effective accountability when battling sexual sin.[57]

- Effective accountability does not rely exclusively on accountability.

- Effective accountability is involved early rather

than late.

- Effective accountability involves someone with maturity.
- Effective accountability involves someone with authority.[58]
- Effective accountability should avoid explicit details.[59]
- Effective accountability places the responsibility for confession on the person with the problem.
- Effective accountability must actually hold people accountable.

Lambert concludes with these words:

> You will not experience dramatic change in your struggle as long as you use accountability to describe your sins instead of declaring your need for help in the midst of temptation.[60]

When David needed help, he sought out Samuel. So it is significant that a chapter that details David's budding relationship with Abigail (another man's wife), begins with the phrase, "Now Samuel died."[61] Without effective accountability, David became increasingly vulnerable.

Several years ago, while attending a conference, I ran into a man who had been a student of mine 20 years earlier. While his hair was graying at the temples, I could still see the youthful 18-year-old lurking behind his eyes. He smiled as we talked—the smile of one who was remembering God's faithfulness as he tried to compress two decades of ministry into a couple of minutes. Suddenly, he stopped in mid-sentence, as if the telling of his story had summoned up a conversation from our past. Thoughtfully, he continued, "Over twenty years ago, you taught me a word, one that I have lived by and that has helped me be faithful to my wife, and my family. It has allowed me to continue in ministry when my friends have fallen out." He paused again, perhaps remembering a close brush with moral failure, or imagining how different his life would have been without that one word. Tears of gratitude were forming as he continued, "Accountability. You taught me about accountability. Thank you." That day, I asked Kevin if I could include his story when I spoke and taught on this subject; a few weeks later, I received it. Here it is in his words.

It was the first time I had told anyone but God about my struggles. We didn't talk about temptations in my church and we certainly didn't talk about them in my family.

I was introduced to the concept of "accountability" during my year at Word of Life Bible Institute in Schroon Lake, New York. The staff had decided to separate the men and women to address gender specific challenges related to purity.

I still have the booklet that we used that night. Our campus pastor had put together the material that taught a Biblical plan for sexuality and strategies for maintaining purity. The booklet also included verses that we were encouraged to memorize to combat temptation.

As we returned to our dorm room that night, my friends and I began to talk openly about the purity struggles that we were experiencing in our lives. We spent some time in prayer for one another and I remember being encouraged to know that I wasn't the only one struggling.

That night, I began the discipline of maintaining accountability relationships, a discipline that I have practiced in my life and ministry for the last twenty-five years. I discovered that although my intentions to live in holiness may be genuine, my sinful heart at times proves to be stronger than my intentions. This may not be true for everyone, but for me, isolation is suicide. I have purposed to never live my life under the radar. I don't want to be able to hide any sin. Every two weeks my accountability partner and I ask each other a series of very specific questions related to pride, sexual purity, materialism, faithfulness in ministry, and faithfulness in our homes. We all need a Nathan to pound his finger into our sternum and say, "You are the man!" (2 Sam. 12:7).

I am thoroughly convinced that, without these relationships, I would have drifted deeply into the shadows of my own sinfulness and would be living life under the radar. For nearly twenty years, God has allowed me to experience victory in areas of my life where I thought victory was unattainable.

By God's grace, the discipline of accountability has been a tool to aid in the sanctifying work of the Holy Spirit in my life. I have come to the conviction that accountability isn't just a good idea, it is part of God's plan to sanctify His church.

Stay on the radar and walk in the light; don't sacrifice your integrity. If you haven't found your Nathan, it's not too late; he is probably looking for you too.

THINK LIKE GOD THINKS
And God Said
(The Nature of Sexual Desire)

ERHAPS YOU can remember the first time you had a sexual thought or desire. Didn't it seem like it was your discovery? While you may have only been curious at first, something inside of you awakened and your mind continued to return to it. Even if somebody else introduced you to the knowledge, when you later thought about it, it seemed like it was your secret—like you were the first person to discover it.

The first untruth: Because sex is something you experience, it feels like it is your idea.

Sexual desires have the potential to affect multiple aspects of your human existence. They bring physical stimulation, emotional pleasure, and—within the context of marriage—spiritual oneness.[62] In many ways, sexual thoughts and desires feel like your personal property. After all, you might reason, they take place in *my* mind, and affect *my* body. It's true. They are your intimate feelings and personal experiences. But that does not mean the idea originated with you.

In my pastoral counseling I have found that most people are surprised to learn that both gender and sex were God's ideas. Often the counselee will look at me stunned; as if *God* and *sex* shouldn't be in the same book, let alone the same sentence. But when you open a Bible, you will see that God isn't bashful about the subject. He introduces these topics in the first four chapters of the first book of the Bible. In those pages, he gives vital principles that have existed from the foundation of time—long before our present day culture's norms came into existence.

Human beings were created in God's image
—male and female

In Genesis chapter 1 we read, "So God created man in his own image, in the image of God he created him; male and female he created them."[63] In one verse, God makes clear two truths about the creation of human beings: (1) that there is a spiritual aspect to each of us—we were made in the image of God; and (2) that the different genders were God's idea—he created us male and female.

Being made in the image of God is a game-changer. It sets us apart from all the other creatures in the animal kingdom. Human beings possesses the capacity to reason morally, not just respond instinctively. Nowhere is this truth more clearly expressed than in the area of our sexual desires. We are not simply animals that respond instinctively to certain pheromones and stimuli; we are beings made in the image of God. As such, we have the ability to think and reason in order to make choices. Sex is not an if-it-feels-good-do-it choice, it is a moral one. The Bible teaches that sexual desires were a gift that God gave to the first couple that he created. The two genders, male and female, were determined by him and assigned at the point of their creation. Sex was not our idea, it was God's. Experimenting outside of his divine plan is not the way to find fulfillment—it's simply a path to disobedience.[64]

Marriage is God's design for the sexual experience

In Genesis chapter 2 we read the following:
Therefore a man shall leave his father and his mother and hold fast to his wife, and they shall become one

flesh. And the man and his wife were both naked and were not ashamed.[65]

Moments after the creation of Eve, God ordained marriage as a relationship between one man and one woman for life. Thousands of years later, Jesus confirmed this principle when he referenced the Genesis passage in his teaching,[66] adding, "What therefore God has joined together, let not man separate." By God's design, marriage—an act of relational commitment—is to be a prerequisite to the sexual relationship. We notice that this first husband (Adam) and wife (Eve) were naked and unashamed. While I have counseled many who feel shame for their past or present moral failures, within the parameters of marriage there is no intended shame. Marriage was designed to be a place of protection—where intimacy on a physical, emotional, and spiritual level could be experienced.

Moral choices incur consequences

As we turn to Genesis chapter 3 we read further:
To the woman he [God] said, "I will surely multiply your pain in childbearing; in pain you shall bring forth children. Your desire shall be for your husband, and he shall rule over you." And to Adam he said, "Because you have listened to the voice of your wife and have eaten of the tree of which I commanded you, 'You shall not eat of it,' cursed is the ground because of you; in pain you shall eat of it all the days of your life."[67]

Because the human race was created in the image of God, capable of moral choice, when Adam and Eve made a wrong moral choice, there were naturally consequences that followed their decision to do what God had warned them not to do. God had previously warned them not to eat from the tree of the knowledge of good and evil,[68] so he was justified in following through with his warning for their sin. The discipline from God's hand meant that they would face pain and, ultimately, death. Those consequences would be passed on to each of us;[69] because, we too, when confronted with the opportunity to choose right or wrong, chose the latter.[70] Instead of following God's design, each of us reaches for what we believe will bring the greatest pleasure in the shortest time possible. While this is the case with all sin, it is especially evident in the realm of sexuality.

There are serious consequences for practicing our sexual desires outside of the marriage relationship. Some of the physical consequences, like sexually transmitted diseases, are irreversible and can result in death.[71] But there are also emotional, relational, and spiritual consequences as well. Because we are moral creatures, created in the image of God, the guilt we feel is real, as are the emotional scars that affect us and others. Few things can scar the trust in a marriage like sexual unfaithfulness. Furthermore, studies have proven that ongoing use of pornography seriously hinders our ability to build meaningful, long-lasting relationships.[72]

Sex is intended to be mutually enjoyed in the marriage

Finally, in Genesis, chapter 4 we read this:

Now Adam had sexual relations with his wife, Eve, and she became pregnant. When she gave birth to Cain, she said, "With the Lord's help, I have produced a man!"[73]

God's design for sex—between a man and woman, within the confines of the marriage relationship—included it being mutually good and enjoyable. It was not forbidden by God, it was encouraged by him. This was what was meant by the command "be fruitful and multiply and fill the earth."[74] There is only one way to keep that command, and the birth of Cain was testimony that Adam and Eve took God seriously.

Within the first few pages of the Bible, we learn that the two genders as well as sexual activity within marriage were God's ideas. Within the parameters of God's design, sexual activity is both commanded and encouraged. However, when you first experience those desires, it still feels like they are yours. This leads us to the second deception we need to consider.

The second untruth: Because sex feels like it's your idea, you believe it's yours to practice as you please.

If sex was God's idea, it would be best to practice it within the parameters he provides. While it may feel like those desires—being fueled by our imaginations and fantasies—are happing to us, God will hold us accountable for them because they are attached to our choices. Whether a thought, an attitude, or an action, the Bible offers a sobering reminder that, when we choose these desires continually, they are not only habit-forming, but also enslaving:

> Don't you realize that you become the slave of whatever you choose to obey? You can be a slave to sin, which leads to death, or you can choose to obey God, which leads to righteous living.[75]

The rightness or wrongness of a thing—in this case, a sexual desire—is not determined by how I feel, but by God's intended design.

Few places in Scripture make this distinction as succinctly as 1 Corinthians chapters 6 and 7. These two chapters offer some of the clearest biblical material to understand God's perspective on the sexual relationship.

- In chapter 6 we see what is forbidden; in chapter 7 we

see what is approved by God.

- In chapter 6 we read about sex outside of marriage; in chapter 7 we read of sex within the marriage.
- In chapter 6 we see imperfect desires; in chapter 7 we see God's perfect design.

Notice what God said in 1 Corinthians 6:

> Or do you not know that the unrighteous will not inherit the kingdom of God? Do not be deceived: neither the *sexually immoral*, nor idolaters, nor *adulterers*, nor men *who practice homosexuality*, nor thieves, nor the greedy, nor drunkards, nor revilers, nor swindlers will inherit the kingdom of God. And such were some of you. But you were washed, you were sanctified, you were justified in the name of the Lord Jesus Christ and by the Spirit of our God [emphasis added].[76]

In the above passage, there are three sexual activities that are not a part of God's design and are forbidden for the believer: sexual immorality, adultery, and homosexuality.

- Sexual immorality translates the Greek word *porneia*. It is a broad, sweeping term used to describe all sexual activity that is expressly forbidden by God.[77] Our English language combined this Greek word *porneia*, with another Greek word, *grapho*, which means "to carve or engrave." The two terms together aptly describe *pornography* as engravings or images of sexual immorality. The image, however, is not the only thing being engraved. Those images, when viewed repeatedly, become engraved in our memory. Like pictures in a vault, they stand ready in your mind to awaken and feed illicit sexual desires.
- Adultery describes the violation of the marriage vows

by a married man or a married woman with someone who is not their spouse. A friend of mine was fond of saying that sex in marriage is a like a fire in the fireplace. It is warm, inviting, and romantic. But sex outside of the marriage is like starting the fire in the middle of the living room. It will burn the house down.

- Homosexuality describes the sexual involvement with a member of the same sex in active thought,[78] desire, or action. The term the *ESV* translates as "homosexuality" in 1 Corinthians 6:11 is a combination of the two Greek terms *malakos* and *arsenokoites* and "refers to the passive and active partners in consensual homosexual acts."[79] To choose to participate either actively or passively is sin. We must maintain a distinction between one individual who struggles with same-sex attraction, and another who is feeding his or her same-sex desires by viewing pornography, entertaining fantasies, or by engaging in relationships or sexual activity. The first is the temptation, the latter is the sin.

While these three immoral sexual desires are forbidden elsewhere in the Scriptures, in 1 Corinthians 6 they are accompanied with a strong warning: *those who practice them will not inherit the kingdom of God.*[80] The lesson in this passage is clear: *just because it feels like sex was our idea, doesn't mean we can practice it as we please.*

Fortunately, even if you have moral failures in your past or are presently struggling with sexual temptation, you are not left without hope. God follows the warning with a promise: change is possible. The apostle Paul writes, "And such were some of you. But you were washed, you were sanctified, you were justified in the name of the Lord Jesus Christ and by the Spirit of our God."[81] In the first century, the receivers of the Corinthian letter lived in a city filled with prostitution and sexual immorality.[82] The phrase "and such *were* some of you" [emphasis added] was a promise of hope that change was possible. They may have participated in the city's immoral activities and carried the accompanying scars of guilt and shame. But Paul reminded them (as he does us) that the Gospel offers the hope of lasting change.

The good news that Jesus died in our place breaks both the penalty and the power of sin. The three words used in the earlier passage—washed, sanctified, and justified—confirm that truth.[83] Of those three words, the word "justified" is my favorite. It bears eternal implications. When we repent and believe that Jesus died on our behalf,[84] a transaction takes place in heaven. The transaction is called *justification.* Because Christ lived a sinless life, his execution could pay the penalty for those of us who had sinned. Justification means that our sin was put toward Jesus' account, and his righteousness was put toward ours. Spiritually speaking, we really are a new creation in Christ.[85] True hope is found in this idea. Whatever wrong desires we had acted out in our past are forgiven, and whatever new desires we hope to develop—for the glory of God—are possible. As a believer, you now have the capacity to do more than continue in your sin. The gospel message reminds us that we are free from those besetting sins.

God's design for sex within marriage

We live in a culture where sex is self-centered. In our society, your desires, feelings, passions, and personal pleasure are expected to take the highest priority. God's design for sex within the marriage, however, is not to be me-based. It is to be others-based.

Notice how God speaks in 1 Corinthians 7:

> But because there is so much sexual immorality, each
> man should have his own wife, and each woman
> should have her own husband. The husband should
> fulfill his wife's sexual needs, and the wife should
> fulfill her husband's needs. The wife gives authority
> over her body to her husband, and the husband gives
> authority over his body to his wife. Do not deprive
> each other of sexual relations, unless you both agree
> to refrain from sexual intimacy for a limited time so
> you can give yourselves more completely to prayer.
> Afterward, you should come together again so that
> Satan won't be able to tempt you because of your
> lack of self-control.[86]

My sexual desires were created, not simply to be gratified,
but so that I can be the recipient of my spouse's serving as I
concentrate on serving her. This approach seems counter-
intuitive to our culture's teaching, but it makes sense in
light of the teaching of Scripture on every other subject. As
Christians, we are to be servants in all aspects of our life—
just like Jesus. Note these passages:

- But whoever would be great among you must be your
  servant, and whoever would be first among you must
  be slave of all. For even the Son of Man came not to be
  served but to serve, and to give his life as a ransom for
  many.[87]

- Have this mind among yourselves, which is yours in
  Christ Jesus, who, though he was in the form of God,
  did not count equality with God a thing to be
  grasped, but emptied himself, by taking the form of a
  servant.[88]

After years of counseling couples, I have found that a serve-
at-all-cost attitude is what gives the sexual act its integrity.

Real love is not found in the physical act of love-making, but in a servant-attitude that touches all other aspects of your marriage. When someone believes that you have their best interest in mind, they are more willing to trust you. True emotional, spiritual, and physical intimacy will happen more naturally in a servant context than in a merely sexual one. G.K. Chesterton made the same point:

> Sex . . . produces an institution; and it is positive and not negative, noble and not base, creative and not destructive, because it produces this institution. That institution is the family; a small state or commonwealth which has hundreds of aspects, when it is once started, that are not sexual at all. It includes worship, justice, festivity, decoration, instruction, comradeship, repose. Sex is the gate of that house; and romantic and imaginative people naturally like looking through a gateway. But the house is very much larger than the gate. There are indeed a certain number of people who like to hang about the gate and never get any further.[89]

In marriage, each spouse should develop broader patterns of selfless living, looking out for the other's needs and not their own. Sex is merely one application of that principle.

Incidentally, even though the Bible does not directly address self-gratification (i.e. masturbation, use of pornography), it is still a wrongful use of our sexual desires. At its core, this practice places you first, not your spouse. Your focus becomes selfish, not selfless. Even if you could detach masturbation from lustful thoughts, pornography, and fantasizing, it would still be unable to accomplish the greater purpose of serving your spouse and allowing them to serve you. On the contrary, it further develops and encourages a selfish expression of your sexual desires—the very thing the culture assumes and that God's design contradicts.

For the unmarried, the practice of self-gratification averts God's preparation for marriage and weakens an essential element of the Christian's life: self-control.[90] Furthermore, after years of counseling married couples, I have learned that masturbation during their single years did not prepare them for marriage. Rather, it only made them more vulnerable to the practice within their marriage: weakening their resolve while strengthening the enemies of intimacy, such as secrecy, selfishness, mistrust, and betrayal.

The third untruth: If it feels right, it must be right.

Throughout this chapter, I've attempted to introduce you to key biblical passages that inform and often contradict our culture's understanding of sexuality. This final untruth is deeply engrained in our culture. In most parts of the world today, it is assumed. It is powerfully deceptive. You've probably heard it before. *If it feels right, it must be must be right.*

On the evening of July 16, 1999, John F. Kennedy Jr. was returning from the wedding of a cousin, flying his Piper Saratoga. Accompanying him that night were his wife, Carolyn, and his sister-in-law, Lauren. The weather report claimed the sky was hazy, providing a challenge for those who weren't accustomed to flying with instruments only. While Kennedy had experience as a pilot, he had not yet acquired his instrument rating. Being unable to view the horizon on a dark and cloudy night made him extremely vulnerable to something known as spatial disorientation. Spatial disorientation is the inability of a person to correctly determine his/her body position in space.[91] With both feet planted firmly on the ground, this is a non-factor: what we feel is confirmed by what we see. But put that same person in an airplane on a dark and cloudy night and it's easy to confuse the organs of equilibrium in the inner ear. Literally, the pilot won't know which way is up. If you don't rely on your instruments on a cloudy night, you court disaster. Even experienced pilots can become spatially disoriented. I've heard of those who flew into a cloud right side up and flew out of it upside down. The inner ear is dependent on the eyes to confirm which way is up. Experienced pilots have learned that they can't trust what they feel, so when they can't see the horizon, they focus instead on their instruments.

Investigators believe that when Kennedy came out of the cloud, his plane was already in the death spin. The crash was inevitable. I've had pilots tell me that you actually have to *will* yourself to trust the instruments. The urge to give into what you're feeling is that strong. Every good pilot knows what the rest of us need to learn: *just because it feels right, doesn't mean that it is right.* The tragedy of Kennedy's death illustrates our societal misunderstanding of sexual desire. We believe something is right because of what we feel. Kennedy's confidence in what he felt was catastrophic—costing him his life and the lives of his loved ones.

Living in the haze of a postmodern culture, we have become sexually disoriented—trusting our feelings instead of the clear direction found in God's Word. Like Kennedy's plane, our lives could be in a tailspin and we wouldn't even know. The Bible works like the pilot's instruments: it discerns the truth.[92] The sexual desires that you and I feel will insist they can be trusted. But things aren't right just because they feel right. On page 62, you will find ten lies that accompany sexual temptation and ten biblical passages that speak truth into those temptations. That's a good place to start learning how to read your truth instruments so that you're ready on a dark and cloudy night.

DO WHAT JESUS DID

Circa 32 AD

I T WAS A DAY that started like any other. The morning gray was seeping through the window as I pulled myself from the bed that was my place of business.[93] I stared out the window of the brothel and longed for something more. But such longings didn't last. Hope had long ago died in this dungeon I called life. I was twelve-years-old when they took me from my home, and a decade had passed since my first transaction. Who was I kidding? Today would be like any other. *You act like you want them, they act like they want you. They slip a copper coin in the dish and the solicitor takes his cut. Repeat the process. Repeat the process. Repeat the...*

The solicitor's voice interrupted my thoughts, "Time to get back to work." I sighed and repeated the sequence: *you act like you want them, they act like they want...* But before the transaction could be completed, three men burst though the door. A disdainful voice scoffed, "Caught her in the very act, we did!" The men wore the robes of the religious leaders—after a decade in this business, you recognized your clients' garments. Roughly, they thrust my hands together, tying them tight before they dragged me into the street.

My solicitor's voice echoed behind me, "That wasn't part of the deal!" They ignored his complaints and hurried me through alleyways of Jerusalem. We had an appointment. Ahead of us I spotted a gathering of those familiar religious robes. They pushed me through the crowd and threw me to the ground. The voice of disdain spoke again: "Teacher, this woman was caught in the very act of adultery! Moses told us we should stone a woman like this. What do you say?"

Time froze. The question hung in the air. The place

48

reeked of their arrogance. Their judgment was palpable. I could hardly breathe, fearing the judgment of this silent teacher. My eyes were locked on the stone in front of me. I expected, at any moment, his hand would reach for it. To meet his eyes was out of the question—that would certainly break his silence and bring his judgment. He was kneeling before me, drawing with his finger in the sand. Suddenly, he spoke, his voice gentle, probing the hearts of my accusers:

"Let him who is without sin among you be the first to throw a stone at her."

Silence again. Longer this time. I waited. Still staring at that stone in front of me, I heard the rustling of robes behind me. The arrogance was dissipating. Only the teacher's humility remained.

"Woman, where are they? Has no one condemned you?"

"No one, Lord."

He was kneeling again. This time his hand reached towards me. Gently, he lifted my head until my eyes met his. Looking into his eyes, I was convinced of the sincerity of the words that followed.

"Neither do I condemn you; go, and from now on sin no more."

To do what Jesus did you must see what Jesus saw

Jesus saw people differently than we do. When the disciples saw children as a nuisance; Jesus saw them as citizens of heaven.[94] When the religious leaders saw the tax-collectors as despicable; Jesus saw them as reachable.[95] And when men saw prostitutes as disposable; Jesus saw them as redeemable—women in need of healing and forgiveness.[96]

Learning to see others as Jesus saw them is an effective means to stand against sexual temptation, both in thought and action. Jesus didn't see people as sex objects to be desired. He saw them as human beings, made in the image of God, broken and in need of healing.

On occasion I have counseled parents whose daughters were dancers in gentleman's clubs. The image the parents gave was not one the paying clientele saw. Their daughters were broken women, struggling with bouts of fear and anxiety. They loathed their career, but lacked the confidence to believe they could do anything else with their lives. They depended on drugs to dull the pain they felt when they took the stage. Their stories were full of sadness. My heart broke as I listened to their parents tell the real story behind the stage personality.

Learning to see others the way that Jesus saw them takes into account the brokenness of those who have been sexually abused. Studies have shown that before the age of 18, one out of every six men and one out of every four women will have experienced sexual abuse. Those numbers are staggering. When I speak on this subject at conferences, I will typically have the men who were born the first two months of the year stand. Then I'll have the women join them who were born the first three months of the year. Then I tell the audience, those standing represent statistically the number of men and women in a crowd of this size that were sexually abused. I'm always amazed at how many people are standing. Those in the audience grow quiet as they come to grips with the pain that has been caused by uncontrolled sexual desire. This is what it means to look at others through the eyes of Jesus.

A friend of mine learned to look through Jesus' eyes on a global scale. In many parts of the world, sex-trafficking runs rampant. Women and children are taken from their homes in rural villages with the promise that there are good paying jobs in the cities. Once they arrive in the city, they are locked in brothels and forced to work the sex trade. My friend understood that unless they were given an additional work opportunity and taught a different trade, they would be caught in an endless cycle. He and his wife discovered a brothel in Asia that covered two city blocks and housed 20,000 women and children who were available to the highest bidder. He grew so burdened that he and his wife packed up their belongings and started a business down the street from the brothel. Slowly, but surely they did what others before them have attempted: rescuing these women by teaching them a respectable trade and providing a safe place for them to survive.

This is what it means to look through the eyes of Jesus. We don't see sex objects to be desired. We see broken people in need of healing and forgiveness.

To do what Jesus did you must think like Jesus thought

In the Sermon on the Mount, Jesus raised the bar on all sorts of issues: anger, anxiety, love, prayer, and giving to name a few. But when he raised the bar on sexual temptation, he must have caused more than a few jaws to drop. Look at what he said:

> You have heard that it was said, "You shall not commit adultery." But I say to you that everyone who looks at a woman with lustful intent has already committed adultery with her in his heart. If your right eye causes you to sin, tear it out and throw it away. For it is better that you lose one of your mem-

bers than that your whole body be thrown into hell. And if your right hand causes you to sin, cut it off and throw it away. For it is better that you lose one of your members than that your whole body go into hell.[97]

Undoubtedly, there were those who heard Jesus' words that day who had not committed the act of adultery, but it's doubtful that there were many who hadn't thought about it. Jesus singled out adulterous thoughts as the culprit. He knew that every sexual action was first preceded by a desire, and each desire was fueled by thoughts. Because we are moral creatures endowed with a choice, our thoughts don't just happen unconsciously—we choose what we think about.[98] Granted, those thoughts can happen so quickly that we forget they are choices—particularly when they are repeated thoughts we have previously dwelled upon. They begin to feel instinctive, like the base sensations other creatures in the animal kingdom experience. But man is different than the animals. As moral creatures, we choose to dwell on certain thoughts that are either right or wrong.

So how do you drive those habitual, sinful thoughts from your mind? In his book *How to Say No to a Stubborn Habit*, Erwin Lutzer writes the following:

> Try this simple experiment. Think of the number eight. Have you visualized it? If so, exercise your willpower and stop thinking of the number eight right now.
>
> Were you able to do it? Of course not. At least, I'm still thinking about that number. Can we, by sheer willpower, stop thinking about the number eight? By no means. Trying to push it out of our minds actually causes us to focus our attention on it.

What a picture of us when we try to overcome sin. We may get on our knees and ask God to take the desire away; we then determine not to think those lurid or greedy thoughts, but there they are again. We resist them once more, trying desperately to push them out of our minds. But we are trapped. Try as we might, we just can't get them to budge.

Can we really be free? Yes, we can control those thoughts, but not by trying to stop thinking about them! To simply resist evil is to make it grow stronger. Our determination not to think lustful thoughts only reinforces them in our thought patterns.

How, then, can we be free? Let's return to our experiment once more and think of the number eight. Although we can't stop thinking about it by sheer resistance, we can push that number out of our minds quite easily. Here's how: Think about one or two bits of information about your mother. Reminisce about your place in the family, whether you are still connected with it or disconnected. Concentrate on this new information, and you'll stop thinking of the number eight.[99]

God gave us a new paradigm of thoughts to press out the old ones. We find it in Philippians 4:8:

> Finally, brothers, whatever is *true*, whatever is *honorable*, whatever is *just*, whatever is *pure*, whatever is *lovely*, whatever is *commendable*, if there is any *excellence*, if there is anything *worthy of praise*, think about these things [...] and the God of peace will be with you [emphasis added].[100]

This passage provides an excellent replacement list for your thinking. You now have eight new qualities to dwell upon that can replace their sinful antitheses.

Go to biblicalstrategies.com, click the resource tab, and you will find a stop-sign graphic with a chart to assist you in training yourself to think new thoughts. The stop sign serves as a visual reminder in the development of new thought patterns. As our minds dwell upon righteous qualities, the unrighteous ones are crowded out.

Jesus' example is a powerful reminder for how we stand against sexual temptation. We must see our minds as the primary battlefields and train ourselves to see others differently—that is, to think of how we can serve them instead of using them for our own benefit. In that way, we will grow to walk just like Jesus.[101]

LIVE BY THE SPIRIT

W HEN THE Bible speaks of the Spirit's role in our battle with sin, it uses the present tense— meaning it is something that must be experienced today. When it comes to sexual temptation, how I wish it would have used the past tense—as in, *I used to struggle with sexual temptation, but the Spirit gave me victory 15 years ago.*

Instead, we are encouraged to be "filled with the Spirit" *today*. In *Just Like Jesus*, I explained our role in this process:

> To be full of the Holy Spirit is to be under his control. This "filling" was not only true of Jesus and Steven; it should be true of all who are believers. Paul gives an even clearer understanding of the Spirit controlled life in his letter to the Ephesians. He writes, "And do not get drunk with wine, for that is debauchery, but be filled with the Spirit.
>
> When someone has had too much to drink, we say that they are no longer "in control." By becoming intoxicated, they have chosen to relinquish their control to another substance. This is the meaning behind the word *filled*. Paul warns us not to be "under the control" of alcohol, but rather to be "under the control of the Holy Spirit."
>
> He carefully chose the verb "be filled" to reveal four essential elements about our relationship with the Holy Spirit. Each of these is hidden in the Greek grammar. Among other things, the Greek language communicates the meaning of its verbs through mood, form, voice, and tense. When it comes to being filled with the Spirit, consider:
>
> ## (1) This isn't Optional.
>
> "Be filled" is in the imperative mood. The impera-

tive mood is one of command. When our mom gave a command, we knew it wasn't optional. God wanted us to know that being filled with the Spirit is not optional, so he chose the mood of command.

(2) This is for All of Us.

"Be filled" is in the plural form. Being filled with the Spirit is not simply for a few – the spiritually elite or hyper-religious – it is a command given for each of us. No one is excluded from this command, so God chose the "all-inclusive" plural form.

(3) This Happens to Us, Not by Us.

"Be filled" is in the passive voice. The active voice is the doer of the action, but the passive voice is the receiver of the action. Imagine I am holding a pitcher filled with water and you are holding an empty glass. If you wish for your glass to be filled, as I begin pouring the water from the pitcher, you don't fill your glass; you simply move your glass so that I can fill it. This isn't simply true of pitchers and glasses. It is true of our relationship with the Spirit; he does the filling, we do the obeying. When we are submitting to his will through our obedience to the Word, we are doing our part. We can trust the Spirit to do his.

(4) This is a Repeated Event.

"Be filled" is in the present tense. Some have properly translated it "be being filled." The present tense implies a daily, moment-by-moment, repeated event. I remember an old preacher who once said he needed to be filled with the Holy Spirit every day because he leaked! That's a good reminder for all of us.[102]

PRIORITIZING THE FIVE STONES

O N THE DESK in my office sits a large glass jar. Its contents, while simple, are unique. People often ask me about its significance. I tell them that it serves as my daily reminder of a story that I heard years ago.

On the first day of the school year, a philosophy professor addressed his students from behind his desk. On its surface, there was a jar containing three large rocks with its lid screwed down tight. He asked his students if they believed he could get anything else in the jar. Unanimously, they agreed he could not. The professor loosened the lid and poured in a jar of pebbles, which rattled their way in and around the larger rocks. He tightened the lid, and taught his lesson.

The next day, he opened his class by drawing their attention to the very same jar. Again, he asked his students whether they thought the jar could hold anything more. Again, they responded that it could not. The professor loosened the lid, and this time took out a container of sand. The students watched as the sand sifted its way down around the pebbles. The professor tightened the lid and taught his lesson.

On the third day, the professor once again took out the jar. He passed it around for the students to examine. They could see the sand and a few of the pebbles, though the larger rocks were now mostly obscured. The professor asked the students if the jar could only anything more. Having viewed it closely, they assured him it could not. The professor loosened the lid, and poured in a glass of water, which gurgled its way down to the bottom of the jar.

The professor tightened the lid, studying his students over the top of his spectacles. He smiled as he asked, "And what is the lesson we can learn about our lives from this small experiment?"

One student raised his hand, desiring to answer the professor's question. "Even if your life is full, you can always get a little more in." The class nodded in agreement.

The professor's smile faded, a reflective furrow creasing his brow. "The lesson we learn..." he paused as if in thought. "Is that your life will soon be filled with small, insignificant details. So you better get your big rocks in first."

The large glass jar that sits on my desk has five large rocks surrounded by numerous smaller ones. To me, this is a daily reminder that there are five qualities that must be developed and maintained if I am to stand against sexual temptation.

I invite you to join me in the battle.

To walk in **humility** is to recognize that you cannot win the battle with sexual temptation in your own strength.

To practice **integrity** is to make a commitment to transparency during temptation, and to confession after sin.

To desire **loyalty** is to love God by using your body for his glory, not your temporary pleasure.

To exercise **responsibility** limits your opportunity for temptation as you are preoccupied fulfilling your commitments.

To live with **accountability** is to guard your vulnerabilities through the Word and fellow believers.

How to Apply What You've Learned

The discovery of new truths is the beginning of change, but discovery by itself cannot accomplish real change. To do that, you will need to replace your old habits with new ones, your old ideas with more accurate ones, and your old thoughts with more biblical ones. The final pages of this booklet are dedicated to helping you establish those new habits. Prayer, Scripture and the Holy Spirit were the divine resources that Jesus used, and those same resources are available to you and me today.

(1) Prayer

Whatever the struggle, we have a tendency to see prayer as a panic button—we hit it only when we're in need. Yet, the Bible has over 650 examples of prayer. These are an excellent resource for growth in your prayer life. You will find the 10-minute prayer pattern on the following page. Additional prayer patterns are available at biblicalstrategies.com under the resources tab.

(2) Scripture

A growing understanding of humility, integrity, loyalty, responsibility and accountability will help us stand against sexual temptation. I have provided 35 days of Bible readings in these areas. To aid with Scripture retrieval, I have included 20 biblical passages to memorize that apply directly to sexual temptation.

(3) The Spirit

Dependence on the Spirit is essential for maintaining our sexual purity. Developing new habits by walking in the Spirit is the means through which we express that daily dependence. You will find key scriptures and key steps for the "fives stones" at the close of the book.

The 10 Minute Prayer Pattern: PRAY

The *PRAY* acrostic is a memory device for prayer. It can be as short as a few minutes or may include more time as God leads. PRAY stands for **P**raise, **R**epent, **A**sk, and **Y**ield.

(1) Praise

At the beginning of prayer, praise the *who*, *what*, and *why* of God. Remember *who* he is by reflecting upon his character. When you remember *what* he's done, you are meditating on his works. Finally, remember the *why* of God. He is motivated by his steadfast love towards us (Psa. 100:5).

(2) Repent

Once you've thought about what God has done, you can move easily to what *you* haven't done. Repentance takes place when we remember our failures and turn from them. A humble confession in prayer reveals a dependence on the Spirit in order to be restored to God. True repentance includes both my actions *and* my attitudes (Phil. 2:5).

(3) Ask

Jesus taught us to *ask* of God, and Paul gave us a great prayer list to follow (see Col. 1:9-12). The prayers of Scriptures are helpful models for learning to pray spiritually for yourself and others.

(4) Yield

Jesus grew to the point where he could say, "Not my will but yours be done." Yielding your desires to God's (as hard as that may initially be) is an essential element of prayer. Once you've made known your requests, make sure you surrender your desires.

35 Daily Bible Readings for Temptation

These readings focus on the five stones of humility, integrity, loyalty, responsibility, and accountability. For further study, there are additional passages on these qualities found on pages 66-74.

DAILY BIBLE READINGS

Humility

Day 1: Mark 9:33-37
Day 2: 2 Corinthians 12:5-12
Day 3: Luke 22:24-27
Day 4: Philippians 2:1-12
Day 5: John 13:1-20
Day 6: Isaiah 53:1-12
Day 7: 1 Peter 5:5-6

Integrity

Day 8: Joshua 7:19-21
Day 9: Psalm 41:11-13
Day 10: Proverbs 2:6-8, 20-21
Day 11: Proverbs 6:16-20
Day 12: Proverbs 16:13, 28
Day 13: Romans 2:21-24
Day 14: Ephesians 4:15, 25

Loyalty

Day 15: Deuteronomy 6:1-5
Day 16: Psalm 73:25, 26
Day 17: Matthew 10:37-39
Day 18: Matthew 22:34-40
Day 19: John: 14:15-24
Day 20: John 15:12-14
Day 21: Philippians 3:7-9

Responsibility

Day 22: Ecclesiastes 3:1-15
Day 23: Matthew 25:14-30
Day 24: Matthew 25:31-46
Day 25: Romans 14:1-21
Day 26: Colossians 3:18-25
Day 27: Romans 12:1, 2
Day 28: Hebrews12:1-11

Accountability

Day 29: Genesis 4:1-16
Day 30: 1 Samuel 18:1-5
Day 31: Ecclesiastes 4:9-12
Day 32: Philippians 2:19-30
Day 33: Galatians 6:1-10
Day 34: James 5:13-18
Day 35: Mark 10:42-45

The Scripture Retrieval Method

The Scripture retrieval method is based upon three premises: (1) Scripture provides an excellent *defense* against temptation. This is why the first ten verses listed below are learned in the lie/truth formula to defend against temptation. (2) Scripture provides an excellent *offense* to weaken temptation's appeal. This is why the second ten verses are learned about the character of God and the nature of the Gospel. Loving God well and appreciating the Gospel weakens the draw of temptation. (3) We learn the Scriptures best when we *understand* the words we are memorizing and *apply* them to our real life challenges. For this reason, memory alone is an ineffective means of defending against sin.

Biblical Truths to Combat the Deceiver's Lies

Lie 1: No one will ever know what you are about to do. Go ahead. No one is watching. Truth: Hebrews 4:13

Lie 2: This temptation is too difficult. Go ahead give in. Truth: 1 Corinthians 10:13

Lie 3: You keep failing. You'll never have victory over this sin. Truth: Philippians 1:6; 4:13

Lie 4: Your past is too bad. You can't overcome it. Truth: Philippians 3:13-14

Lie 5: You can't change. That's just the way you are. Truth: 2 Corinthians 5:17

Lie 6: Marriage shouldn't matter. Sex is OK if you love each other. Truth: Hebrews 13:4

Lie 7: You can avoid the consequences. Your situation is unique. Truth: Job 31:11-12 NLT; Galatians 6:7-9

Lie 8: It's your body—you should be able to do as you please. Truth: 1 Corinthians 6:18-20

Lie 9: You can overcome this sin alone. Don't tell anybody. Truth: James 5:16; Psalm 32:3-5

Lie 10: If it feels right it must be right. Truth: Ephesians 4:22-24

Biblical Promises about God and the Gospel

Promise 1: God is good, loving, and faithful. Passage: Psalm 100:5

Promise 2: God loves me and enjoys acting on my behalf. Passage: Zephaniah 3:17

Promise 3: God sacrificed his Son to show his love for me Truth: Romans 5:8, 10

Promise 4: Nothing can separate me from the love of God. Passage: Romans 8:35, 37

Promise 5: God is purposefully at work in my life and circumstances. Passage: Jeremiah 29:11, 13

Promise 6: God will be with me in my trials. I am not alone. Passage: Isaiah 43:2

Promise 7: God will strengthen me when I am weak. Passage: Isaiah 41:10, 13

Promise 8: God is near when I'm in trouble. Passage: Psalm 46:1-2

Promise 9: Having been forgiven, I need not fear God's condemnation. Passage: Romans 8:1

Promise 10: God saved me because of who he is, not because of who I am. Passage: Titus 3:4-6

Visit biblicalstrategies.com to order these 20 memory verse cards with helpful commentary on the back of each card.

Suggestions for Scripture retrieval: defense & offense

Walking in the Spirit

The Bible uses the word *walk* to communicate the daily choices we are making. Those choices become habit-forming, eventually shaping our lives and defining our future. As believers, the Holy Spirit empowers our ability to make new choices—as opposed to simply repeating the same old patterns of behavior. This is why Paul wrote, "Walk by the Spirit, and you will not gratify the desires of the flesh" (Gal. 5:16). A practical way to do this is to choose the Spirit's fruit over your flesh's desires. Look closely at the following two lists. Identify the "desire of the flesh" with which you are most likely struggling (Gal. 5:19-21). Consider which item from the "fruit of the Spirit" list would be its most likely replacement (Gal. 5:22-23).

REPLACEMENT LIST Fruit of the Spirit
Love
Joy
Peace
Patience
Kindness
Goodness
Faithfulness
Gentleness
Self-control

DESIRES LIST Works of the Flesh
Sexual immorality
Impurity
Lustful pleasures
Idolatry
Sorcery
Hostility
Quarreling
Jealousy
Outbursts of anger
Selfish ambition
Dissension
Division
Envy
Drunkenness
Wild parties

(1) Identify the struggle

To identify the struggle, ask good questions around the five W's. *When* are you most likely to be tempted?

What circumstances surround your engagement in sinful desires? *Who* are you with when you're tempted? *Why* are you susceptible to this temptation—are there underlying motives you haven't considered? *Which* desire from the "works of the flesh" list is your greatest struggle?

(2) Replace the desire with the fruit

Once you have identified the struggle, look to the fruit of the Spirit and indentify the replacement. For example: replace fits of anger with patience, jealousy with joy, selfish ambition with love, hostility with gentleness, and so forth.

(3) Study and apply the truth

Once you've chosen the item from the fruit of the Spirit list, study it. You can use a topical Bible to locate other biblical passages where the word is explained. Develop an understanding using another author's insight.[170] Write a workable definition of the word.[171] Now, apply those definitions to your specific situation. For instance, perhaps you need patience with your kids, peace with your spouse, or love for your fellow employee. Review the definition in advance of the challenge. Imagine various scenarios that could take place, then mentally practice your response.

(4) Repeat the process for permanence

Practice doesn't make perfect. Practice makes *permanent.* As you have practiced giving into the "deeds of the flesh," you have developed those desires into habits. Reversing that order will take time, but it is possible by the Spirit's power. This is why *walking* is an excellent metaphor for how we grow in the Spirit. Step by step, we learn new patterns of thinking, choosing, and living.[103]

To walk in **humility** is to recognize that you cannot win the battle with sexual temptation in your own strength.

Key Scriptures on Humility

2 Chronicles 7:14
Proverbs 11:2
Proverbs 12:15
Proverbs 18:12
Proverbs 22:4
Psalm13:1
Psalm 147:6
Ecclesiastes 5:2
Jeremiah 9:23
Micah 6:8
Matthew 5:3
Matthew 23:12
Mark 9:33-37
Mark 10:44, 45
Luke 14:10, 11
Luke 22:24-27
John 3:30
Romans 11:18
Romans 12:3, 10
2 Corinthians 11:30
2 Corinthians 12:5-12
Ephesians 4:2
Philippians 2:1-12
Colossians 3:12
1 Peter 3:8
1 Peter 5:5, 6
James 4:6, 10

Key Scriptures on Pride

Jeremiah 9:23
Obadiah 1:3
Proverbs 8:13
Proverbs 12:15
Proverbs 16:5, 18
Proverbs 21:24
Proverbs 25:14, 27
Proverbs 26:12
Proverbs 27:2
Proverbs 29:23
Proverbs 30:12
Matthew 23:10-12
Romans 11:17-21
Romans 12:2, 3, 16
Romans 15:17
1 Corinthians 13:4
2 Corinthians 10:12, 31
2 Corinthians 12:7
Galatians 6:3
Philippians 2:3
1 Timothy 6:4
2 Timothy 3:2
James 4:6
1 Peter 5:5
1 John 2:16

Key steps

- *Pay more attention to your own faults than the flaws of others.*

Prideful people are often critical of others. Give greater consideration to the areas in your own life that need improvement. Ask God for wisdom and seek legitimate input from loving friends. Ask them for areas where you could improve.

- *Dwell upon the attributes of God.*

Consistent study of the character of God aids in proper understanding of yourself. You may download at 30-day listing of the attributes of God at biblicalstrategies.com under the resources tab. Meditate on one of God's attributes daily for 30 days and then repeat the process.

- *Practice a regular time of prayer and fasting.*

Prayer and fasting allow you to live in a moment-by-moment dependence on the Lord. Fasting allows you to regularly recognize your physical weakness. Praying consistently reveals our neediness before the Lord.

- *Create a thanksgiving journal.*

Maintaining a regular list of relationships, items, and events for which you are grateful creates an attitude of thanksgiving and a posture of humility. When your grateful spirit is growing, you are less prone to develop the sense of entitlement that is so prevalent with sexual temptation.

- *Develop a servant-spirit.*

Look for ways to serve others without expecting anything in return. Opportunities to serve that go unnoticed are especially good opportunities to develop humility. Remember, the hardest part about being a servant is being treated like one. Allow those moments to knock off the prideful edges as you learn to walk in humility.

Suggestions for developing humility

To practice **integrity** is to make a commitment to transparency during temptation, and to confession after sin.

Key Scriptures on Integrity

1 Kings 9:4-5
Psalm 25:19-21
Psalm 26:1-3; 8-12
Psalm 41:11-13
Proverbs 2:6-8; 20-21
Proverbs 10:9
Proverbs 11:1, 3
Proverbs 16:13, 28
Proverbs 19:1
Proverbs 12:22
Job 2:3
Matthew 5:37
Luke 16:10-12
John 8:32
Acts 24:16
Romans 2:21-24
2 Corinthians 8:21
Galatians 6:7-8
Ephesians 4:15, 25
Philippians 4:8-9
Colossians 3:9
Hebrews 13:8
1 Peter 3:10-12
1 John 1:9

Key Scriptures on Deceit

Genesis 20:5-6
Exodus 20:16
Joshua 7:19-21
Psalm 101:7
Proverbs 6:16-20
Proverbs 11:1
Proverbs 12:19, 22
Matthew 15:18-20
Luke 8:17
John 8:43-47
Ephesians 4:25
Colossians 3:9-10
James 1:26
James 3:14
1 Peter 3:10-12
1 John 2:4

Suggestions for developing integrity

Key steps

- *Work at being the same person in public as you are in private.*

Those who repeatedly fall to sexual temptation have learned to live two different lives—one public and one private. Try to bring your private persona in line with who you show yourself to be when you're with others.

- *Expect to be tested.*

Integrity, like many other character qualities, must be tested to be revealed and refined. Expect to face temptations to not tell the truth. Tempting opportunities to lie, cheat, and withhold the truth are chances to instead reveal that you are walking in integrity.

- *Maintain relationships where you can share transparently when you're tempted.*

Struggles with sexual temptation are generally private. Work hard to maintain several relationships where you can maintain a level of honest transparency during the times you're tempted. In order to reach out to them for prayer and Scriptural support when you're tempted, you'll need to develop the relationship when you're not.

- *Confession after you've sinned should be vertical and, when necessary, horizontal.*

Whenever we've committed sexual sin, we have sinned first and foremost against God (2 Sam.12:13; 1 Cor. 6:18, 19). Start your confession there, but also consider if there is someone else you may have sinned against in the process; i.e. your spouse (1 Cor. 7:4), employer (Col. 3:22, 23), etc. Confession to God is essential; confession to others is often more humbling.

To desire **loyalty** is to love God by using your body for his glory, not your temporary pleasure.

Suggestions for developing loyalty

Key steps

- *Meditate on God's love for you, and you'll find that you will love him more.*

We can never fully grasp the love of the Creator for his creation. His love is truly amazing. Imagine God the Father's conversation with God the Son. Reflect upon his willful surrender to die in your place. Ponder the suffering of the cross. In your free time, think about his love for you; you'll find that you will love him more.

- *Remember the cost of your freedom.*

The Scriptures say, "knowing that you were ransomed from the futile ways […] not with perishable things such as silver or gold, but with the precious blood of Christ" (1 Peter 1:18-19). Reviewing daily the cost of your freedom weakens the draw of sexual temptation.

- *Think of specific ways your "ransomed" body can be used for God's glory.*

Don't simply think of "not sinning." Consider the ways that you can reflect the glory of God. Develop replacement attitudes and actions for your sinful ones. It may be helpful to place the specifics of these "God-glorifying" tasks on a list. As you complete the list you will be creating new habits and developing new desires.

- *Study the glory of God in the Scriptures and in creation.*

The Psalms are an excellent Biblical resource for voicing the glory of God. Dwelling upon the attributes and character of God will increase your understanding of his glory. There is a 30-day listing of his names and attributes at biblical-strategies.com under the resource tab. Reflecting upon the work of God in creation is another way to study his glory, and it will help you to see you and your desires in perspective.

To exercise **responsibility** limits your opportunity
for temptation because you are preoccupied
fulfilling your commitments.

Your Role	Key Biblical Passages
Ambassador	Pr. 13:17; 2 Co. 5:20; Ep. 6:20; Jn. 20:21
Church Member	1 Co. 12:12-27; Ro. 12:1-8; Ep. 4:12-16
Citizen	Mt. 22:20-22; Ac. 22:25-27; Ep. 2:19; Ph. 3:20
Disciple	Mt. 10:34-38; Mk. 10:17-27; Lu. 9:23-27; 14:27
Employee	Ge. 2:15; 3:17-19; Pr. 21:25; 1 Th. 2:9; Co. 2:23
Employer	Pr. 22:16; Je. 22:13; Ep. 6:9; Ja. 5:4
Example	1 Co. 11:1; Ro. 14:1-21; 1 Th. 1:5-7; 1 Ti. 4:12
Friend	Pr. 17:17; 27:17; 18:24; Jn. 15:13; Ph. 2:3-8
Husband	Ge. 2:18, 24; Ep. 5:25-33; Co. 3:19; 1 Pe. 3:7
In-law	Ge. 2:24; Ex. 18:1-27; Ru. 1-4
Leader	Mk. 10:42-45; Ph. 2:5-8; 1 Ti. 4:12; 2 Ti. 2:2-26
Man	Jos. 1:8; Ep. 6:1-13; 1 Co. 6;13-14; 1 Jo. 2:6
Neighbor	Pr. 3:29; Mt. 7:12; Lk. 10:25-37; Ro. 15:2; Ja. 2:8
Parent	De. 6:6-9; Ps. 127:3; Pr. 13:24; Co. 3:21; He. 12
Peace keeper	Ps. 34:13-14; Mt. 5:9; He. 12:14; Ja. 3:17-18
Servant	Mt. 25:35-40; Mk. 10:44-45; Ga. 5:13-14
Steward	De. 8:17-18; Mt. 25:14-30; 1 Co. 4:2; 1 Pt. 4:10
Sufferer	Is. 53:3-10; Ac. 9:16; He. 12:2; 1 Pe. 4:12-16; 5:10
Teacher	Ez. 7:10; Lk. 6:40; Ja. 3:1; Tit. 2:7; 2 Ti. 2:24-26
Temple	Ro. 12:1; 1 Co. 3:16-17; 6:19-20; 1 Ti. 4:7-9
Wife	Ge. 2:18; 1 Pe. 3:1-6; Pr. 18:22; 31:10-31
Woman	Ru. 3:11; Pr. 14:1; 31:30; Titus 2:3-5; 1 Pt. 3:1-6

Suggestions for developing responsibility

Key steps

- *Seek God's direction through prayer.*

Start by talking to God. He desires for you to trust him and seek his guidance (Pro. 3:5-6). He wants you to know his will so that you might do it (1 Thes. 4:1-3). Focus on an attitude of submission: you want to do whatever he reveals.

- *Ponder your roles and responsibilities.*

Think about the roles and responsibilities to which God has called you. Most often these will be expressed in the context of your relationships (friend, employee, mother, daughter, etc.). List them. They will become the foundation for the next step.

- *Discover key Scriptures that inform your identity.*

I recommend these tools to find key Biblical passages: a topical Bible, concordance, *The Treasury of Scripture Knowledge*, or *The Quick Scripture Reference for Counseling*. You can also search the internet by entering "What does the Bible say about (fill in your role)."

- *Develop identity statements based upon what you discover when studying Scripture.*

Try to delineate your role to one sentence, or it may simply be 3-5 key words. Keeping it concise is the first step to making it memorable. It will need to be memorable if you are to apply it in daily decision-making.

- *Make decisions in light of your identity statements.*

Before you commit to a new task or responsibility, check your identity statements. Does this decision fall in line with what God has called you to do? Does it enhance your Biblically derived identity or distract from it? Review the identity statements often, until you've developed the habit of living by them.[104]

Taken from *Taking Back Time: biblical strategies for overcoming procrastination*

Suggestions for developing accountability

The chart is an extrapolation of Heith Lambert's 7 statement on accountability. It offers helpful ideas on the nature of ac countability. Chart developed by Tim Challies at challies.com

Accountability Is	Accountability Is...	Accountability Is Not...
1. Effective accountability does not rely exclusively on accountability.	...one weapon among many.	...the only weapon in the fight against sin.
2. Effective accountability is involved early rather than late.	...calling out for help in the moment of temptation and *before* you sin.	...delayed confession—the regular reporting of sins already committed.
3. Effective accountability involves someone with maturity.	...able to function best when it occurs under the leadership of someone who has a track record of victory over the sin in question.	...going to work well if you are seeking accountability with someone who is struggling and sinning in the same area as you.
4) Effective accountability involves someone with authority (Heb 13:17).	...involving those who can speak with authority. It may also involve those who "...watch over you as those who must give an account."	...fighting on your own; by definition, accountability is not a solo effort.
5) Effective accountability should avoid explicit details (Eph 5:11-12).	...describing sin and temptation in general terms with the goal of enabling your accountability person to help you best.	...not a place where explicit details are shared; we must avoid fueling further temptation.
6) Effective accountability places the responsibility for confession on the person with the problem.	...full and free confession without prompting, pushing or demands for honesty.	...going repeatedly through a list of questions without making honest and up-front confession of a particular sin
7) Effective accountability must actually hold people accountable.	...being actively involved in the life of another Christian with regular and caring communication.	...simply the commitment to meet regularly and work through a list of questions.

NOTES

1. Malcolm Gladwell, *David and Goliath* (New York, NY: Black Bay Books, 2013), 300.

2. 1 Samuel 17:46, 47

3. This narrative is my imaginative retelling of the actual events. The historical records are found in 1 Samuel 17 and 2 Samuel 11.

4. 1 Samuel 16:7

5. Genesis 39:10, 12, NLT

6. 1 Samuel 16:18

7. 1 Samuel 18:7

8. 1 Samuel 17:46-48

9. 1 Samuel 17:33-36

10. Proverbs 6:26

11. 1 Corinthians 6:17, NLT

12. 1 Timothy 6:11, NLT

13. 2 Timothy 2:22, NLT

14. 1 Corinthians 10:12

15. Randal Roth, *Prayer Powerpoints* (Wheaton, IL: Victor Books, 1995), 210.

16. 1 Samuel 23:2, 4, 11, 12; 30:8; 2 Samuel 2:1, 2; 5:19, 23; 21:1.

17. Psalm 18:1, 2

18. http://www.foxnews.com/tech/2015/08/19/hackers-say-theyve-posted-data-adultery-website-ashley-madison-users-online.html

19. Psalm 32:2-4

20. Psalm 32;1, 5

21. 1 Samuel 18:11; 19:11

22. 1 Samuel 18:29

23. 2 Samuel 20:6

24. 1 Samuel 21:1

25. 1 Samuel 22:9, 10

26. Psalm 32, 51

27. Psalm 51:10, 12

28. W.E. Vine, *Vine's Complete Expository Dictionary of Old and New Testament Words* (Nashville, TN: Thomas Nelson, 1996), Vol. 1, 187.

29. R. Ellsworth, *Opening up Psalms* (Leominster: Day One Publications, 2006), 72–73.

30. 1 Samuel 17:37, 46

31. *The MacArthur Study Bible* notes, "The multiplication of David's wives and concubines was in direct violation of Deut. 17:17. These marriages reflected David's involvement in international treaties and alliances that were sealed by the marriage of a king's daughter to the other participants in the treaty. This cultural institution accounted for some of David's and many of Solomon's wives (see 1 Kin. 11:1–3). In each case of polygamy in Scripture, the law of God was violated and the consequences were negative, if not disastrous" (John MacArthur, *The MacArthur Study Bible* (Wheaton, IL: Crossway Books, 1997), 434).

32. David showed a special interest in all three women while they were married to another man: Abigail was married to Nabal (1 Sam. 25), Michal was married to Paltiel (2 Sam. 3), and Bathsheba was married to Uriah (2 Sam. 11).

33. 2 Samuel 11:24

34. Proverbs 4:23, NLT

35. 1 Corinthians 6:18-20

36. 1 Samuel 11

37. 1 Corinthians 6:19

38. J.R.R. Tolkien (New York, NY: Harper Collins Publishers, 1995), 576.

39. Romans 12:1, 2, NLT

40. 2 Samuel 11:1, 2, NLT

41. Matthew 5:27, 28; Proverbs 23:7, KJV

42. The *Four Rules for Purity* are: (1) you can't fight the battle alone and win; (2) you can't fight the battle without a sword—scripture memory is important; (3) free time is enemy territory; (4) free sex is a lie—it's not free, it's a chain.

43. Colossians 3:18-21

44. Colossians 3:20-24; 4:1

45. Ephesians 6:8; 1 Corinthians 7:3

46. Colossians 4:2-6

47. Luke 10:36-37

48. Psalm 19:8, 9; 11-13

49. Hebrews 4:12

50. Don Whitney, *Spiritual Disciplines* (Colorado Springs, CO: Navpress, 1991), 44.

51. 1 Samuel 18:3

52. 1 Samuel 20:33

53. 2 Samuel 1:25-26. *The ESV Study Bible* adds this helpful note: Jonathan deeply loved and supported David (as seen in 1 Sam. 18:1–20:42; 23:16–18), in accordance with their covenant with the Lord. [The phrase] "surpassing the love of women" [...] does not carry any sexual overtones. Rather, he is calling attention to Jonathan's radical self-denial in giving up any right to the throne of Israel (1 Sam. 23:17); instead, he gave his absolute support to David as the Lord's choice to succeed Jonathan's father Saul, even to the point of risking his life for David. (*The ESV Study Bible*, (Wheaton, IL: Crossway Publishers, 2008), 544).

54. 1 Samuel 16:7

55. 1 Samuel 19:18

56. 1 Chronicles 9:22

57. Heith Lambert, *Finally Free: fighting for purity with the power of grace* (Grand Rapids, MI: Zondervan, 2013), 45-57.

58. Hebrews 13:17

59. Ephesians 5:11, 12

60. Heith Lambert, *Finally Free: fighting for purity with the power of grace* (Grand Rapids, MI: Zondervan, 2013), 49.

61. 1 Samuel 25:1

62. 1 Corinthians 7:1-5

63. Genesis 1:27

64. Romans 1:28-32

65. Genesis 2:24-25

66. Matthew 19:4

67. Genesis 3:16-17

68. Genesis 2:17

69. Romans 5:12

70. Our choice of sin is a result of our sinful nature. Theologian Paul Enns explains: "Sin is a principle within man. Sin is not only an act but also a principle that dwells in man. Paul refers to the struggle with the sin principle within (Rom. 7:14, 17–25); all people have this sin nature (Gal. 3:22). Hebrews 3:13 refers to it "as the power that deceives men and leads them to destruction." Jesus also refers to sin as a "condition or characteristic quality"(John 9:41; 15:24; 19:11) (Paul Enns, *The Moody Handbook of Theology*, (Chicago, IL: Moody Press), 310).

71. Sexually Transmitted Diseases (STD) can have life and death consequences. Consider the following report: "There is a strong connection between sexually transmitted diseases and cancer of the cervix. Human papillomavirus types 16 and 18

(as well as other less common HPV types) are causes of precancerous changes in the cervix and cervical cancer. The strongest predisposing factors in cervical cancer are a history of intercourse at an early age and multiple sexual partners" (http://answers.webmd.com/answers/1171176/what-is-the-correlation-between-sexually).

72. covenanteyes.com/2015/12/29/how-porn-is-keeping-men-from-marriage/

73. Genesis 4:1, NLT

74. Genesis 2:28

75. Romans 6:16, NLT

76. 1 Corinthians 6:9-11

77. *The MacArthur Study Bible* adds this note: "The Gr. word is porneia, from which the Eng. word "pornography" comes. It refers to all illicit sexual activity, including (but not limited to) adultery, premarital sex, homosexuality, bestiality, incest, and prostitution" (John MacArthur, *The MacArthur Study Bible* (Wheaton, IL: Crossway Books, 1997), 544).

78. On the issue of homosexuality and the Christian's response, I strongly recommend Peter Hubbard's work *Love into Light: the gospel, the homosexual and the church.* Dr. Fred Zaspel writes about this book, "Powerfully insightful...I am not aware of a more valuable "first resource" to help shape our thinking on this very contemporary issue" (Peter Hubbard: *Love into Light*, Greenville, SC: Ambassador International, 2013).

79. Description referenced in the margin of the *English Standard Version.*

80. *The Macarthur Study Bible* adds, "The kingdom is the spiritual sphere of salvation where God rules as king over all who belong to Him by faith. All believers are in that spiritual kingdom, yet are waiting to enter into the full inheritance of it in the age to come. People who are characterized by these iniquities are not saved (v. 10). While believers can and do commit these sins, they do not characterize them as an unbroken life pattern. When they do, it demonstrates that the person is not in God's kingdom. True believers who do sin, resent that sin and seek to gain the victory over it" (John MacArthur, *The MacArthur Study Bible* (Wheaton, IL: Crossway Books, 1997), 1736).

81. 1 Corinthians 6:11

82. "The distinctive cult of Corinth was veneration of Aphrodite, goddess of love, beauty, and fertility, who is identified with the Roman Venus. The summit of Acrocorinth was dominated by a temple dedicated to her worship, served by over 1,000 sacred prostitutes or slave-priestesses. Associated with such religious practices was a general moral degradation. Corinthian morals were notoriously corrupt, even when compared with pagan Rome" (W.A. Elwell, *Baker Encyclopedia of the Bible*, (Grand Rapids, MI: Baker Book House, 1988), 514).

83. Dr. Wayne Grudem gives these definitions: "Sanctification is a progressive work of God and man that makes us more and more

free from sin and more like Christ in our actual lives. Justification is an instantaneous legal act of God in which he (1) thinks of our sins as forgiven and Christ's righteousness as belonging to us, and (2) declares us to be righteous in his sight" (Wayne Gurdem, *Systematic Theology*, (Grand Rapids, MI: Inter-Varsity Press, 2004), 1253, 1736.

84. Romans 10:11

85. 2 Corinthians 5:17

86. 1 Corinthians 6:2-5, NLT

87. Mark 10:44-45

88. Philippians 2:5-7

89. G.K. Chesterton, *G.K.'s Weekly*, January 29, 1928.

90. Galatians 5:22, 23

91. http://www.faa.gov/pilots/safety/pilotsafetybrochures/media/spatiald.pdf

92. Hebrews 4:12

93. This narrative is my imaginative retelling of the events. The biblical story is found in John 8:1-11.

94. Matthew 19:14

95. Luke 19:1-10

96. Luke 7:36-50

97. Matthew 5:27-30

98. Proverbs 23:7, KJV; James 1:15-16

99. Erwin Lutzer, *Getting to No* (David C. Cook, 2012-01-17. iBooks).

100. Philippians 4:8

101. This is the thought behind *Just Like Jesus: biblical strategies for growing well.*

102. ibid., 43-44

103. Originally published in *Dead-End Desire: biblical strategies for overcoming self-pity*, 68-69.

104. Originally published in *Taking Back Time: biblical strategies for overcoming procrastination*, 70-71.

About Biblical Strategies

Biblical Strategies exists to provide resources for those who desire to change, but need help taking the next steps.

- The series is comprised of brief booklets that explain and apply Biblical passages to a specific struggle.

- The accountability plan helps the reader overcome the temptation by implementing the key growth habits of prayer, Scripture memory, daily Bible readings, and application of truth.

- The Scripture Retrieval System is a memory aid in which Biblical passages have been selected for each temptation. Ten passages expose temptation's deception; the remainder weaken temptation's appeal as truths about the character of God and the nature of the gospel are committed to memory.

About 12th Man Training

12th Man Training is character-based instruction for men using the Biblical Strategies material. Biblical help is offered in 30, twenty-minute teaching segments as men develop biblical strategies for overcoming the issues with which they often struggle — anger, self-pity, sexual temptation, procrastination, anxiety, and broken relationships. These sessions are offered for free online. Go to the blog at biblicalstrategies.com and select 12th Man Training.

A unique aspect of the training is the directed table-talk discussions. For 35 minutes following the teaching, a table leader fosters discussion around that week's topic, provides accountability for each man's spiritual growth, and builds community among the men at the table.

About the Author

Phil Moser is the author of the Biblical Strategies series. He is a pastor, frequent blogger (philmoser.com) and conference speaker. He holds a degree in Business Management, and earned his Masters of Divinity from The Master's Seminary, Sun Valley, California. He presently serves as the teaching pastor of Fellowship Bible Church in Mullica Hill, New Jersey. He has served as an adjunct professor teaching the Bible, theology, apologetics, homiletics, and counseling in Albania, Korea, Germany, Hungary and Ukraine.

Resources from Biblical Strategies

Just Like Jesus: biblical strategies for growing well

Fighting the Fire: biblical strategies for overcoming anger

Dead End Desire: biblical strategies for overcoming self-pity

Taking Back Time: biblical strategies for overcoming procrastination

Safe in the Storm: biblical strategies for overcoming anxiety

Strength for the Struggle: biblical strategies for standing against sexual temptation

Biblical Strategies
How you get to where God's taking you.
BiblicalStrategies.com